MAY
CAUSE
HAPPI-
NESS

ABOUT SOUNDS TRUE

Sounds True is a multimedia publisher whose mission is to inspire and support personal transformation and spiritual awakening. Founded in 1985 and located in Boulder, Colorado, we work with many of the leading spiritual teachers, thinkers, healers, and visionary artists of our time. We strive with every title to preserve the essential "living wisdom" of the author or artist. It is our goal to create products that not only provide information to a reader or listener, but that also embody the quality of a wisdom transmission.

For those seeking genuine transformation, Sounds True is your trusted partner. At SoundsTrue.com you will find a wealth of free resources to support your journey, including exclusive weekly audio interviews, free downloads, interactive learning tools, and other special savings on all our titles.

To learn more, please visit SoundsTrue.com/freegifts or call us toll-free at 800.333.9185.

SOUNDS TRUE
many voices, one journey

ABOUT THE AUTHOR

 avid Steindl-Rast was born
Franz Kuno Steindl-Rast
on July 12, 1926, in Vienna,
Austria. He spent all of his
teen years under the Nazi
occupation and was drafted into the army,
but he never went to the front lines. He
eventually escaped and was hidden by his
mother until the occupation ended.

© DIEGO ORTIZ MUGICA

After the war, Franz studied art,
anthropology, and psychology. He immigrated to the US in the
1950s and joined Mount Saviour Monastery, where he became
"Brother David."

After twelve years of monastic training and studies in
philosophy and theology, Brother David was sent by his abbot
to participate in Buddhist-Christian dialogue. These interfaith
dialogues have continued all his life and resulted in deep friendships
with leaders from all the major world religions. In the early 1960s,
together with Thomas Merton, Brother David helped launch a
renewal of religious life. For decades, Brother David divided his
time between periods of hermit's life and extensive lecture tours
on five continents.

Brother David has brought spiritual depth into the lives of
countless people whom he touches through his lectures, workshops,
YouTube videos and Ted Talks, and writings. His books have been
translated into many languages.

Gratefulness, the Heart of Prayer and *A Listening Heart* have
been reprinted and anthologized for more than two decades. His
most recent books are *Words of Common Sense for Mind, Body,
and Soul*; *Deeper than Words*; *99 Blessings*; *Faith Beyond Belief*;
and his autobiography, *i am through you so i.*

At present, Brother David serves a worldwide Network for
Grateful Living through Gratefulness.org, an interactive website
with several thousand participants daily from more than 240
countries and territories.

MAY CAUSE HAPPINESS

A GRATITUDE JOURNAL

**FROM THE
TEACHINGS OF
BROTHER DAVID
STEINDL-RAST**

SOUNDS TRUE

BOULDER, COLORADO

Sounds True
Boulder, CO 80306

Published 2018

Cover design by Rachael Murray
Book design by Beth Skelley

Cover illustration by Helen Siegl

All text used with permission.

Printed in Canada

ISBN: 978-1-68364-057-8

10 9 8 7 6 5 4 3 2 1

EDITOR'S NOTE

ounds True is delighted to bring you this journal—peppered throughout with quotations from the writings of our dear friend, Benedictine monk Brother David Steindl-Rast, particularly his writings on gratitude and happiness. One of Brother David's core teachings, and one that continues to move us in deep and surprising ways, is that in any given moment life gives us the opportunity to be grateful.

If you have ever kept a journal, you know that a regular writing practice is a wonderful gift, especially when we are feeling stressed or stretched by life. It gives us permission to observe, question, and wrestle with how life works and who we are within it. We live in a world so full of distractions. As Brother David writes in *The Way of Silence*, "Oversaturation of our senses tends to dim our alertness. A deluge of sense impressions tends to distract the heart from single-minded attention. This gives me a new appreciation for the hermitage, a fresh understanding of what solitude is all about. The hermit—the hermit in each of us—does not run away from the world, but seeks that Still Point within, where the heartbeat of the world can be heard."

Regular journaling allows you to find your Still Point—that quiet place within you where your innate wisdom resides—and hear the heartbeat of the world. We think Brother David's extraordinary insights about living with passionate aliveness will aid in your inquiry. (It should be noted that Brother David reviewed the quotations and in some cases changed the wording slightly in order to clarify a point.)

There is no right or wrong way to use this journal. Bring it with you in your bag or briefcase. Pull it out and scribble down a few thoughts as they occur to you, or leave it by your bedside or reading chair and develop (or continue) a regular writing habit. If you have been telling yourself that you never have time to write, pick a regular, convenient time each day or week and commit to writing then. Put it on your calendar or set a reminder on your phone. Just try it and find what works for you.

Brother David's words are added for inspiration. I hope they help unlock your stories, thoughts, and feelings. Sometimes they want to be read more than once, or you may find yourself wrestling with them. You might even want to talk back to the words at the top of a given page. Great. It's *your* journal.

And may you find, as I have through the process of re-reading Brother David's body of writings to select the quotations for this journal, a glimpse of what he means by a sense of "limitless belonging" to this world, an awakened sense of gratitude, curiosity, and awe. As Brother David writes in *Gratefulness, the Heart of Prayer*, "As we learn to give thanks for all of life and death, for all of this given world of ours, we find a deep joy—the joy of courageous trust, the joy of faith in [what Reinhold Niebuhr called] 'the faithfulness at the heart of all things.' It is the joy of gratefulness in touch with the fullness of life."

CAROLINE PINCUS FOR SOUNDS TRUE

BEFORE I TURN
OFF THE LIGHT IN
THE EVENING, I JOT
DOWN IN MY POCKET
CALENDAR ONE
THING FOR WHICH I
HAVE NEVER BEFORE
BEEN GRATEFUL.
I HAVE DONE THIS
FOR YEARS, AND THE
SUPPLY STILL SEEMS
INEXHAUSTIBLE.

BEING IN THE
PRESENCE, BEING
PRESENT, MEANS
A CONTINUOUS
ENCOUNTER WITH
MYSTERY. NOT
ONLY BEING
PRESENT TO
ANOTHER, BUT
BEING PRESENT
TO THE WATER
WE DRINK, AND
TO THE FLOWERS
WE SEE, AND TO
EVERYTHING
THAT COMES
OUR WAY—EVERY
THING, EVERY
PERSON, EVERY
ANIMAL, EVERY
PLANT, EVERY
SITUATION IN
LIFE, OPEN
FOR ENCOUNTER.

On an island in Maine, I once found tidal pools on the granite shore with water so still and clear I could see the fine fibrils of sea anemones on the bottom, waving like festive streamers. Still more limpid is the inner space to which silence is the key. I don't always find that key, but when I do, I simply enter.

God's singing can be as jubilant as the red of God-made tomatoes, as the soaring of a kite or the splashing of children in a pool. But it can also be as heavy as the fragrance of lilies in a funeral home, as heavy as the news of a friend's grief. God's singing can be as light as harpsichord music or a spring outing, as sad as the howling of a night train or the evening news. It can be cheerful, enchanting, challenging, amusing. In everything we experience, we can hear God singing, if we listen attentively.

THERE IS NO
LONGER ANY
DOUBT IN MY MIND
THAT I BELONG
TO THIS EARTH
HOUSEHOLD, IN
WHICH EACH
MEMBER BELONGS
TO ALL OTHERS—
BUGS TO BEAVERS,
BLACK-EYED
SUSANS TO BLACK
HOLES, QUARKS TO
QUAILS, LIGHTNING
TO FIREFLIES,
HUMANS TO
HYENAS AND
HUMUS. TO SAY
"YES" TO THIS
LIMITLESS MUTUAL
BELONGING IS
LOVE. THOSE WHO
SAY THAT GOD IS
LOVE MEAN THIS
KIND OF LOVE,
THIS GREAT "YES"
TO BELONGING.

SILENCE IS THE OPPORTUNITY TO LET YOURSELF DOWN INTO MYSTERY~TO LET YOURSELF BE TOUCHED BY MYSTERY. IT IS LIKE THE JOY OF MUSIC, ONLY A THOUSAND TIMES DEEPER AND GREATER.

THE HEART
IS A HIGHLY
SENSITIVE
RECEIVER;
IT CAN
LISTEN
THROUGH
ALL OUR
SENSES.
WHATEVER
WE HEAR—
BUT ALSO
WHATEVER
WE SEE,
TASTE,
TOUCH,
OR SMELL—
VIBRATES
DEEP DOWN
WITH GOD'S
SONG.

Rightly understood, the mystic is not
a special kind of human being; rather,
every human being is a special kind of mystic.
At least, this is our calling.

Where do we find limitless belonging?
You may have felt it on a mountaintop.
or when listening to music.
But you may just as likely have been
surprised by it when you were stuck
in rush-hour traffic or changing
your baby's diapers. Whenever it hits us.
we know: This is it! This is the answer.
as it were. to a question we keep
carrying around with us. unable
to put it into words and unable
to drop it. We may not be able
to put the answer into words
either—who can put the meaning
of a sunrise into words?—
but we can rest in it.
We have come home.
We have found meaning.

WHEN RELIGIOUS
TRADITIONS SPEAK
OF THE **DIVINE LIFE**
WITHIN US, THEY REFER,
IMPLICITLY AT LEAST,
TO OUR **HIGH POINTS**
OF WAKEFUL AWARENESS,
TO OUR MYSTICAL
EXPERIENCES. YES,
LET US NOT SHY AWAY
FROM THAT THOUGHT.
WE ARE ALL **MYSTICS**.

SOMETIMES WHEN WE ARE
ALONE, WE FIND THAT~NOT
SO MUCH IN SPITE OF BUT
BECAUSE OF BEING SO TRULY
ALONE AT THAT MOMENT~WE
ARE UNITED WITH EVERYTHING
AND EVERYBODY. WHETHER WE
ARE ALONE IN OUR ROOM OR
WITH THE TREES, THE ROCKS,
THE CLOUDS, WATER, STARS,
WIND, OR WHATEVER IT IS,
WE FEEL AS IF OUR HEART IS
EXPANDING, AS IF OUR BEING
IS EXPANDING TO EMBRACE
EVERYTHING, AS IF THE
BARRIERS WERE IN SOME WAY
BROKEN DOWN OR DISSOLVED,
AND WE ARE ONE WITH ALL.
WHEN I AM MOST TRULY ALONE,
I AM ONE WITH ALL.

OFTEN TO FIND THE
ANSWER, YOU HAVE TO
DROP THE QUESTION.
SOMETHING KNOCKS
YOU OVER, AND FOR
A SPLIT SECOND YOU
DROP **THE** QUESTION,
AND THE MOMENT YOU
DROP THE **QUESTION**
THE ANSWER IS THERE.

THE MOMENT YOU HAVE
SAID AN UNCONDITIONAL
YES TO ANY PART OF
REALITY, YOU HAVE
IMPLICITLY SAID YES
TO EVERYTHING; NOT YES
TO EACH SPECIFIC THING,
BUT YES TO EVERYTHING
THAT YOU OTHERWISE PO-
LARIZE INTO GOOD AND
BAD, BLACK AND WHITE,
UP AND DOWN. YOU ARE
NO LONGER SAYING,
"YES, BUT." YOU SIMPLY
SAY YES, AND ALL OF A
SUDDEN ALL OPPOSITES
FALL INTO ONE GREAT
PATTERN, AND YOU HAVE
SAID YES TO THE WHOLE.

There are some who claim not to know gratefulness. But is there anyone who never knew surprise? Does springtime not surprise us anew each year? Or that expanse of the bay opening up as we come around the bend of the road? Is it not a surprise each time we drive that way? What counts on our path to fulfillment is that we remember the great truth that moments of surprise want to teach us: everything is gratuitous, everything is gift.

A complete stranger might pull your sleeve and point to the sky: "Did you notice the rainbow?"

And you become an excited child. You might not even understand what startled you when you saw that rainbow. What was it? Gratuitousness burst in on us, the gratuitousness of all there is. When this happens, our spontaneous response is surprise. Plato recognized that surprise as the beginning of philosophy. It is also the beginning of gratefulness.

WE WORK
UNTIL WE HAVE
ACCOMPLISHED
OUR PURPOSE.
WE SWEEP THE
FLOOR UNTIL IT
IS SWEPT. BUT
WE DON'T SING
IN ORDER TO
GET A SONG
SUNG—WE SING
IN ORDER TO
SING. AND WE
DON'T DANCE,
AS ALAN WATTS
POINTED
OUT, TO GET
SOMEWHERE;
WE DANCE
IN ORDER
TO DANCE.
PLAY HAS ALL
ITS MEANING
IN ITSELF.

EVEN WHEN OUR LIFE
LACKS THE SURPRISE
OF THE EXTRAORDINARY,
THE ORDINARY ALWAYS
WANTS TO SURPRISE US
AFRESH. AS A FRIEND
WROTE TO ME FROM
MINNESOTA ON A WINTER
MORNING: "I GOT UP
BEFORE DAWN AND
CAUGHT GOD PAINTING
ALL THE TREES WHITE.
SHE'S BEEN DOING MUCH
OF HER BEST WORK WHILE
WE SLEEP TO SURPRISE
US WHEN WE GET UP."

To be alive, awake, aware in all
areas of our lives is the task
that is never accomplished, but
it remains the goal. Since we all
know what it means to be alive in
at least one area, we have some
sense of what it must mean to be
ablaze with the Holy Lifebreath
in all of one's life.

The taste
of wild
strawberries,
a toothache, or the
pleasure rippling all
over your skin after
a bath—these are
bodily experiences.
But can you say this
with the same assurance
about homesickness,
faithfulness, or the awe
you feel as you look at
the photograph of the

Andromeda Nebula, two million light years from Earth and 200,000 light years in diameter?

We humans belong to both realms: the realm of the senses and the realm that goes beyond them. But if we deny being animals and neglect or reject our senses, we clip the very wings on which we are meant to rise beyond space and time.

AN INCH
OF **SURPRISE**
CAN LEAD TO
MILES OF
GRATEFULNESS.

From hive to blooming meadow
and back home, our hearts keep
winging their way; from the
invisible through the visible
and then—heavy with harvest,
like bees with baggy pants
of pollen and bellies
bulging with nectar—
back home to Rilke's
"great golden honeycomb
of the invisible." This
is the pattern of our
heart's repeated journeys
throughout life and of life's
quest as a whole.

OUR EYES SEE,
BUT ONLY OUR
HEART LOOKS
THROUGH THINGS
TO FIND THEIR
MEANING. OUR
NOSE REGISTERS
SCENTS, BUT
ONLY OUR HEART
WILL TRACK
LIKE A HOUND
ITS ETHEREAL
QUARRY. OUR
TONGUE TASTES,
BUT ONLY A
HEART CAN
FEAST. SKIN
TOUCHES SKIN,
BUT BEING IN
TOUCH IS A
MATTER OF THE
HEART. OUR
EARS HEAR,
BUT ONLY A
LISTENING HEART
UNDERSTANDS.

THINK ABOUT A MOMENT OF
GREAT ALIVENESS IN YOUR
LIFE, A MOMENT OF REAL
MINDFULNESS ROOTED IN
THE BODY. IT WAS A MOMENT
IN WHICH YOU WERE IN
TOUCH WITH REALITY. WE
CAN MEASURE THE DEGREE
TO WHICH WE ARE ALIVE AND
SPIRITUAL BY
THE DEGREE
OF OUR BEING
IN TOUCH
WITH REALITY.

T.S. Eliot says in *Four Quartets*, speaking about a peak experience: it is "music heard so deeply that it isn't heard at all, but you are the music while the music lasts." You are the music. You vibrate with that music. You might just be thinking of some flute or piano music that you listen to, but it's the music of the universe that you are vibrating to. It's the music to which this whole cosmic dance dances, and that flows through you. That's your religious moment. And in that moment, you know that you are one with all. You are the music while the music lasts, simply that.

IF YOU HAVE NEVER BEEN SURPRISED
THAT YOUR DOG REMAINS SO
DEPENDABLY A DOG AND DOES NOT
SUDDENLY TURN INTO A KANGAROO
OR A HIPPOPOTAMUS, CHANCES ARE
THAT YOU ARE STILL TAKING REALITY
A BIT TOO UNQUESTIONINGLY FOR
GRANTED. ALLOWING OURSELVES
TO BE SURPRISED THAT THINGS ARE
WHAT THEY ARE MAKES US WAKE UP
FROM A DEEP SLEEP. CULTIVATING
SURPRISE WILL DO WONDERS FOR OUR
WAKEFULNESS, OUR ALIVENESS.

THERE IS ONLY ONE
CONDITION FOR
SEEING LIFE AS
A SACRAMENT:

TAKE OFF YOUR SHOES!

REALIZE THAT THE
GROUND ON WHICH
YOU ARE STANDING
IS HOLY GROUND.

ASK YOURSELF, "WHEN DID I, FOR ONE SPLIT SECOND, KNOW THAT I BELONGED—DID I KNOW IT IN MY BONES, THAT I WAS ONE WITH ALL AND ALL WAS ONE WITH ME?"

TO LIVE MEANS TO DIE
WITH EVERY HEARTBEAT
AND WITH THE NEXT
ONE TO BE BORN ANEW;
WITH EVERY BREATH TO
BREATHE OUT WHAT IS
OLD AND TO BREATHE
IN WHAT IS NEW. THIS
DEMANDS COURAGE,
THE COURAGE TO LET GO.
GROWING IS DYING INTO
GREATER ALIVENESS.

Moments of blissful wholeness, moments when we feel one with all, can be triggered by an everyday occurrence, by something we have done a hundred times before. There seems to be no reason why at the hundred and first time it should move us so amazingly, but it does. A mother looks at her baby asleep in the crib countless times a day, yet this time the sight floods her whole heart with a gratefulness too deep for words. Or you drive a stretch of highway twice a day, yet this time the hum of the car, the red-and-white flags at the used car lot, the very ordinariness of the moment seizes your heart with a deep, all-pervading, overflowing sense of gratefulness. This kind of experience pulls us together at a deep level—together with ourselves at our heart of hearts and together with everyone else—intimately at home with ourselves and intimately united with all others.

To light a candle by myself is one of my favorite prayers. There  is the sound of striking the match, the whiff of smoke after blowing it out, the way the flame flares up and then sinks, almost goes out until a drop of melted wax gives it strength to grow to its proper size and steady itself. All this, and the darkness beyond my small circle of light, is prayer. I enter into it as one enters a room.

When we take a hearty
BREATH, we give ourselves
to the AIR we INHALE;
and when we give it out
again, we take a quick
BREAK from BREATHING.
This balance of giving
and taking is the key to
HEALTHY LIVING. It is a
giving within taking and
a taking within giving, a
LIFE-giving GIVE-and-take.

TO BLESS WHATEVER
THERE IS, AND FOR NO
OTHER REASON BUT
SIMPLY BECAUSE IT IS,
THAT IS OUR RAISON
D'ÊTRE; THAT IS WHAT
WE ARE MADE FOR. THIS
SINGULAR COMMAND
IS ENGRAVED IN OUR
HEART.

WHENEVER WE ARE TRULY AWAKE AND ALIVE,
WE ARE ALSO TRULY GRATEFUL.

AS WE LEARN
TO GIVE
THANKS FOR
ALL OF LIFE
AND DEATH,
FOR ALL THIS
GIVEN WORLD
OF OURS,
WE FIND A
DEEP JOY—
THE JOY OF
COURAGEOUS
TRUST, THE
JOY OF
FAITH IN THE
FAITHFULNESS
AT THE
HEART OF ALL
THINGS. IT IS
THE JOY OF
GRATEFULNESS
IN TOUCH WITH
THE FULLNESS
OF LIFE.

THE SURPRISE WITHIN
THE SURPRISE OF EVERY
NEW DISCOVERY IS THAT
THERE IS EVER MORE TO BE
DISCOVERED. HOPE HOLDS
THE PRESENT OPEN FOR
AN EVER-FRESH FUTURE.

For an experience in which our senses spontaneously spark off a grateful response, a footbath is not a bad choice. Your heart and your tongue may not yet be ready, but in their own way your toes will start to sing gratefully. Can anyone deny that this is a step in the direction of "life abundant"?

HOW CAN I GIVE A FULL RESPONSE TO THIS PRESENT
MOMENT UNLESS I AM ALERT TO ITS MESSAGE?
AND HOW CAN I BE ALERT UNLESS ALL MY SENSES
ARE WIDE AWAKE?

Oversaturation of our senses tends to dim our alertness. A deluge of sense impressions tends to distract the heart from single-minded attention. This gives me a new appreciation for the hermitage, a fresh understanding of what solitude is all about. The hermit—the hermit in each of us—does not run away from the world, but seeks that Still Point within, where the heartbeat of the world can be heard.

GRATEFULNESS
BRINGS JOY TO MY
LIFE. HOW COULD I
FIND JOY IN WHAT I
TAKE FOR GRANTED?
THE MOMENT I
STOP "TAKING FOR
GRANTED," THERE
IS NO END TO THE
SURPRISES I FIND.

ounds we like are readily recognized as blessings. But what shall we do when traffic noise does batter our ears? Can we experience this, too, as blessing? One helpful habit I have learned is to refrain as long as possible from identifying unpleasant noises. As long as I manage to simply listen without giving a

name to what I hear—
"squealing brake" or
"ambulance siren"—
I am receiving a pure
sense impression with no
tag attached, no judgment
made. Stripped of all labels,
naked noises are at least
worth our attention. In
this noteworthiness lies a
tiny seed of appreciation,
a seed that might sprout
and grow into a delightful
surprise.

Most people's glorious gates of perception creak on rusty hinges. How much of the splendor of life is wasted on us because we plod along half-blind, half-deaf, with all our senses throttled and numbed by habituation. How much joy is lost on us! How many surprises we miss! It is as though Easter eggs had been hidden under every bush, and we were too lazy to look for them. But it need not be so. We can deliberately pay attention each day to one smell, one sound that we never appreciated before, to one color or shape, one texture, one taste to which we never before paid attention.

EVERYTHING IS A **GIFT.** THE DEGREE TO WHICH WE ARE **AWAKE** TO THIS TRUTH IS A MEASURE OF OUR GRATEFULNESS, AND **GRATEFULNESS** IS A MEASURE OF OUR **ALIVENESS.**

If we are afraid
of making fools of
ourselves, too proud
to lose our balance even
for a moment, too eager
to cut a good figure
in God's sight, we end
up standing there like
statues in dignified
poses and make fools
of ourselves after all.
But readiness to lose our

balance is not enough. If,
in the process, we stumble
all over ourselves, it is
just as foolish. We must
dare to lose our balance,
and yet keep it. We must
dare to make fools of
ourselves but be careful
not to do it foolishly.
Faith is the art of making
fools of ourselves wisely,
like dancers.

A listening heart recognizes, in the throbbing
of reality pulsating against all our senses,
the heartbeat of divine life at the core of
all that is real.

_____

_____

_____

_____

_____

_____

_____

_____

_____

_____

MEANING MUST BE CONSTANTLY RECEIVED, LIKE THE **LIGHT** TO WHICH WE MUST OPEN OUR **EYES** HERE AND NOW, IF WE WANT TO **SEE**.

ISN'T IT SURPRISING
THAT THERE IS ANYTHING
AT ALL, RATHER THAN
NOTHING? LOOK AT
LEAST TWICE A DAY AT
SOMETHING~WHATEVER
IT MAY BE~AND ASK
YOURSELF, "ISN'T THIS
SURPRISING?" BY THIS
SIMPLE METHOD, YOU
WILL BECOME MORE AND
MORE AWAKE TO THE
SURPRISING WORLD
IN WHICH WE LIVE.

THE OPPORTUNITY THAT ANY GIVEN MOMENT OFFERS YOU IS AN OPPORTUNITY TO ENJOY—TO ENJOY SOUNDS, SMELLS, TASTES, TEXTURE, COLORS, AND, WITH STILL DEEPER JOY, FRIENDLINESS, KINDNESS, PATIENCE, FAITHFULNESS, HONESTY, AND ALL THOSE GIFTS THAT SOFTEN THE SOIL OF OUR HEART LIKE WARM SPRING RAIN.

If we didn't have this present moment,
we wouldn't have any opportunity
to do or experience anything at all.

_____

_____

_____

_____

_____

_____

_____

_____

_____

SOMETIMES
IT IS **ENOUGH**
TO BE
GRATEFUL
FOR THE
NEXT **BREATH.**

Yesterday, I found a huge moth on the sidewalk. I did stop long enough to put it in a safe spot on the lawn just a foot away, but I didn't crouch down to spend time with this marvelous

creature. Only faintly
did I remember, at night,
those iridescent eyes on
the grayish brown wings.
My day was diminished
by this failure to stay
long enough with this
surprise gift, to deeply
look at it and savor its
beauty gratefully.

IN ORDER TO OPEN
OURSELVES TO
LIFE, WE NEED
COURAGEOUS TRUST.
THE OPPOSITE IS
FEAR. FEAR CLOSES
US OFF FROM LIFE.
TRUST AND FEAR
ARE THE TWO GREAT
OPTIONS WE HAVE.
EVERYTHING DEPENDS
ON THIS BASIC
CHOICE: "WILL I FEAR
OR TRUST LIFE?"

I'm grateful for questions, especially unanswered ones; they keep me alert.

AS HUMAN
BEINGS,
WE ARE
FREQUENTLY
CONFRONTED
WITH THAT
WHICH WE
CANNOT
GRASP.
WE CANNOT
GET IT INTO
OUR GRIP.
BUT WE CAN
UNDERSTAND
IT BY LETTING
IT GRASP US.

OUR WHOLE PRACTICE
OF GRATEFULNESS
IS A METHOD OF
ALLOWING OURSELVES
TO INTERACT WITH
THE GREAT MYSTERY
THAT IS LIFE.

I remember Swami
Satchidananda saying:
"When you start digging—
keep digging! Because if you
dig a little here and you think,
'Oh, I'm not hitting any water,'
and then you go somewhere
else and start digging there,
you are always digging and
stopping before you dig deep
enough to hit water."

_____

_____

_____

_____

_____

_____

_____

_____

_____

_____

_____

YOU CAN BE
GRATEFUL AT
ALL TIMES BY
ASKING **"WHAT IS
LIFE OFFERING ME?"**
MOMENT BY MOMENT.

WITH BLESSING, THE
STREAM OF LIFE
FLOWS THROUGH
US TO ALL THOSE
WE BLESS. IT COMES
BACK TO US, FLOWS
OUT, COMES BACK
TO US, FLOWS OUT.
BLESSING PLUGS US
INTO THE ALIVENESS
OF THE WHOLE WORLD.

THERE IS NOT ROOM IN THE SAME HEART FOR BOTH GRATEFULNESS AND ALIENATION. WHEN YOU ARE GRATEFUL, YOU KNOW THAT YOU BELONG TO A NETWORK OF GIVE-AND-TAKE, AND YOU SAY "YES" TO THAT BELONGING. THIS "YES" IS THE ESSENCE OF LOVE.

"All is always now," says T. S. Eliot. What a profound insight. Not only is the now not in time; time is in the now. When the future comes, it will be now, and any past event becomes now as we remember it. There is only one now. It cannot be multiplied; it simply is.

WE WILL END THIS BOOK THE WAY BROTHER DAVID OFTEN ENDS HIS TALKS— WITH A FAVORITE PHRASE:

"FEAR NOT!
HAVE TRUST IN LIFE!
FEAR NOT!
AND RUN WITH IT!"

SOURCES FOR FURTHER READING

The following is a list of all the sources used for the quotations in this journal. Those who would like to further investigate Brother David's writings and teachings on gratitude will find any of these a great place to start:

"The ABCs of Grateful Living: A Practice." *A Network for Graceful Living.* gratefulness.org/resource/the-abcs-of-grateful-living-gratitude-alphabet-practice/.

"Anatomy of Gratitude" (transcript). *OnBeing* podcast with Krista Tippett. February 9, 2016. gratefulness.org/resource/anatomy-of-gratitude-transcript/.

Aronson, Martin, introduction by Brother David Steindl-Rast. *Jesus and Lao Tzu: The Parallel Sayings.* Berkeley: Ulysses Press, 2002.

"Awake, Aware, and Alert." *A Network for Graceful Living.* gratefulness.org/resource/awake-aware-and-alert/.

"A Basic Human Approach to Happiness." *A Network for Graceful Living.* gratefulness.org/resource/human-approach-happiness.

"Everyday Mysticism: A Report." *A Network for Grateful Living.* gratefulness.org/resource/everyday-mysticism-life-legacy-br-david-steindl-rast-report/.

The Grateful Heart: A Benedictine Monk and Religious Scholar Explores How to Open Your Heart to the Blessings Awaiting Us. Boulder, CO: Sounds True, 1997.

"Grateful Living in the 'Double Realm.'" *Insights at the Edge* podcast with Tami Simon, April 17, 2016.

Gratefulness, the Heart of Prayer: An Approach to Life in Fullness. Ramsey, NJ: Paulist Press, 1984.

A Listening Heart: The Spirituality of Sacred Sensuousness. New York: The Crossroads Publishing Company, 1999.

Music of Silence: A Sacred Journey through the Hours of the Day. Berkeley: Ulysses Press, 2001.

"Questioning Life and Presence." Talk given at Eckhart Tolle's Living a Life of Presence conference, October 2, 2016.

"A Vision for the World." *A Network for Graceful Living.* gratefulness.org/resource/vision-for-the-world/.

"Want to Be Happy? Be Grateful." Ted Talk, June 2013. ted.com/talks/david_steindl_rast_want_to_be_happy _be_grateful/.

The Way of Silence: Engaging the Sacred in Daily Life. Cincinnati: Franciscan Media, 2016.